The United States

Mississippi

Paul Joseph
ABDO & Daughters

visit us at
www.abdopub.com

Published by Abdo & Daughters, 4940 Viking Drive, Suite 622, Edina, Minnesota 55435. Copyright © 1998 by Abdo Consulting Group, Inc., Pentagon Tower, P.O. Box 36036, Minneapolis, Minnesota 55435 USA. International copyrights reserved in all countries. No part of this book may be reproduced in any form without written permission from the publisher.

Printed in the United States.

Cover and Interior Photo credits: Super Stock, Peter Arnold, Inc., Corbis-Bettmann, Wide World

Edited by Lori Kinstad Pupeza
Contributing editor Brooke Henderson
Special thanks to our Checkerboard Kids–Peter Rengstorf, Peter Dumdei, Laura Jones

All statistics taken from the 1990 census; The Rand McNally Discovery Atlas of The United States. Other sources: Compton's encyclopedia, 1997; *Mississippi*, Heinrichs, Children's Press, Chicago, 1989.

Library of Congress Cataloging-in-Publication Data

Joseph, Paul, 1970-
    Mississippi / Paul Joseph.
    p. cm. -- (United States)
    Includes index.
    Summary: Surveys the people, geography, and history of the state of Mississippi.
    ISBN 1-56239-883-0
    1. Mississippi--Juvenile literature. [1. Mississippi.] I. Title. II. Series: United States (Series)
    F341.3.J67 1998
    976.2--dc21
                                                                       97-22674
                                                                          CIP
                                                                           AC

Contents

Welcome to Mississippi 4
Fast Facts About Mississippi 6
Nature's Treasures 8
Beginnings 10
Happenings 12
Mississippi's People 18
Splendid Cities 20
Mississippi's Land 22
Mississippi at Play 24
Mississippi at Work 26
Fun Facts 28
Glossary 30
Internet Sites 31
Index 32

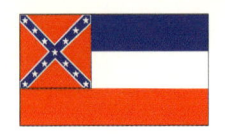

Welcome to Mississippi

The state of Mississippi is in the south-central part of the United States. Mississippi is known as one of the Gulf States because it **borders** the **Gulf of Mexico** in the southeast part of the state.

The state takes its name from the Mississippi River, which flows along the entire western boundary of the state. The name Mississippi is said to have come from **Native American** words that mean "large waters" or "father of waters."

Mississippi could have been called the Cotton State. In the 1700s and 1800s people found that the soil and climate were perfect for growing cotton. It soon became the main **industry** in the state. After the **Civil War**, however, slavery was outlawed. Soon there weren't enough workers to take care of all the cotton.

The Mississippi cotton harvest in the Mississippi River Delta.

Fast Facts

MISSISSIPPI

Capital and largest city
Jackson (196,637 people)

Area
47,234 square miles
(122,335 sq km)

Population
2,586,443 people
Rank: 31st

Statehood
Dec. 10, 1817
(20th state admitted)

Principal rivers
Mississippi River
Pearl River

Highest point
Woodall Mountain;
806 feet (246 m)

Motto
Virtute et armis
(By valor and arms)

Song
"Go, Mississippi"

Famous People
Jefferson Davis, William Faulkner, Elvis Presley, Leontyne Price, Tennessee Williams

*S*tate Flag

*M*agnolia

*M*ockingbird

*S*outhern Magnolia

About Mississippi

The Magnolia State

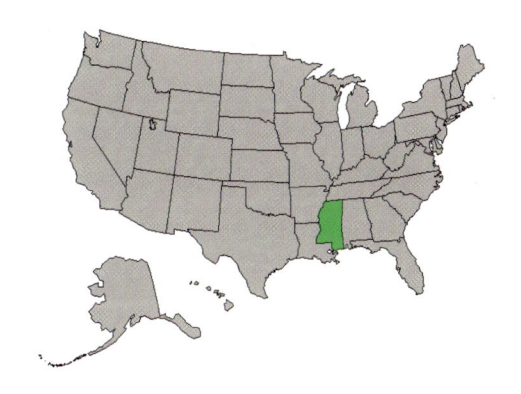

MS
Mississippi's abbreviation

Borders: west (Louisiana, Arkansas), north (Tennessee), east (Alabama), south (Louisiana, Gulf of Mexico)

Nature's Treasures

Mississippi has many treasures in its state. Its land grows many crops that are sent all over the world. Underground, there are many different kinds of **minerals**. The hills, forests, rivers, and **Gulf of Mexico** provide natural beauty and many things to do.

A mild temperature, a good amount of both sunshine and rainfall, and rich soil make Mississippi one of the great cotton-growing areas in the world.

Other farmers throughout the state grow crops such as hay, corn, oats, rice, wheat, and soybeans. Mississippi is one of the states in the country that raises the most chickens.

More than half of the state of Mississippi is covered with forests. With timber **produced** in every area of the state, Mississippi has more tree farms than any other state.

Petroleum is by far the state's most valuable **mineral**. This mineral **produces** gas so people can drive cars and operate other types of engines. Petroleum is found underground in many parts of Mississippi. **Natural gas**, cement, sand, and gravel are also found in Mississippi.

The **Gulf of Mexico** and coastal rivers provide fun in the sun. They also provide many fish that are caught and sold. Some of the fish from Mississippi that people from around the country buy and eat are catfish, shrimp, oysters, and crabs.

An off-shore oil rig near Pascagoula, Mississippi.

Beginnings

The first known people to live in Mississippi were **Native Americans**. The Chickasaw lived in the north, the Choctaw in the center and south, and the Natchez along the lower Mississippi River.

The first **European** to enter what is now Mississippi was the Spanish **explorer** Hernando de Soto in 1540. The French explorer Robert La Salle claimed the area for his country, France, in 1682.

In 1763, the area was under British control. In 1798, the entire state of Mississippi became part of the United States. On December 10, 1817, Mississippi became the 20th state.

By the 1830s, Mississippi was one of the country's richest states because of cotton. Mississippians received a lot of money for their cotton. The plantation owners built huge, beautiful mansions to show off their wealth.

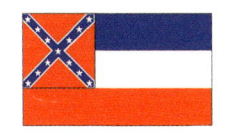

The riches all ended when the American **Civil War** began. This war was between the southern states, who wanted slavery, and the northern states, who wanted to end slavery. The North won the war and many people from Mississippi were killed and much of the state was destroyed.

After the Civil War the time known as Reconstruction began. This was a time when the southern states began to rebuild. It was a slow process, however, the state did prosper again. New crops were planted, railroads were built, the timber **industry** took off, and colleges were started.

A large plantation house near Port Gibson, Mississippi.

Happenings • Happenings • Happenings • Happenings • Happenings • Happen

B.C. to 1540

Early Land and People

During the Ice Age, many thousands of years ago, Mississippi was covered by huge glaciers of ice. Many years later the ice began to melt and the land of Mississippi began to form.

The first known people to occupy Mississippi were **Native Americans**. They were the Chickasaw, the Choctaw, and the Natchez.

1540: Hernando de Soto is the first **European** to explore Mississippi.

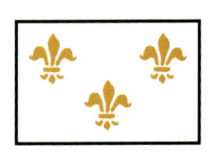

1682: Robert La Salle claims Mississippi for France.

Happenings • Happenings • Happenings • Happenings • Happenings

Mississippi
B.C. to 1540

Happenings • Happenings • Happenings • Happenings • Happenings • Happen

1763 to 1844

Statehood and Beyond

1763: A treaty gives Mississippi to England.

1798: A treaty gives Mississippi to the United States.

1817: Mississippi becomes the 20th state on December 10.

1844: The University of Mississippi is opened.

*penings • **Happenings** • **Happenings** • **Happenings** • **Happenings** • **Happenings***

Mississippi

1763 to 1844

Happenings • Happenings • Happenings • Happenings • Happenings • Happen

1861 to Present

Confederacy to Today

1861: Mississippi leaves the United States. The state joins the Confederate States of America. Mississippian Jefferson Davis is named president of the new country.

1870: Mississippi rejoins the United States.

1927: Mississippi River's worst flood devastates the western part of the state.

1985: Judge Reuben Anderson becomes the first African American Supreme Court Justice in Mississippi.

1988: Mississippi has the worst drought and heat wave in 50 years causing terrible damage to the farm land.

penings • Happenings • Happenings • Happenings • Happenings • Happenings

Mississippi

1861 to Present

Mississippi's People

Many well known people have come from Mississippi. James Meredith was an African American who applied to the all-white University of Mississippi. He was not let in because of people's **prejudices** against African Americans. Finally the Supreme Court ordered that he be allowed into the school.

After riots broke out, the National Guard was called in and he was finally allowed to enter. He graduated and later earned a law degree from Columbia University and became a hero for an entire country.

Medgar Evers was a **civil rights** activist who worked for the NAACP (National Association for the Advancement of Colored People). He was murdered at his home because he fought for equal rights for African Americans. In 1969, Charles Evers, Medgar's brother, was the first African American mayor in the state of Mississippi.

James Thomas Bell was born in Starkville, Mississippi. Bell, who was nicknamed "Cool Papa," was elected to the Baseball Hall of Fame in 1974. He played in the Negro Leagues because in his time African Americans couldn't play in the Major Leagues.

Elvis Presley, known as the "King of Rock and Roll," was born in Tupelo, Mississippi in 1935.

Mississippi is also home to some of the most famous authors the United States has **produced**. Among them were William Faulkner, Tennessee Williams, Eudora Welty, Willie Morris, Shelby Foote, and Richard Wright, who wrote the books *Black Boy* and *Native Son*.

James Howell Meredith    *Tennessee Williams*    *William Faulkner*

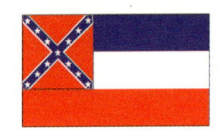

Splendid Cities

Mississippi has many splendid cities in its state. Only one city in the state has more than 100,000 people. Most cities in Mississippi are small in **population** but still have many things to do and see.

The state capital and largest city in Mississippi is Jackson. Jackson is an **industrial** city in the south-central part of the state with close to 200,000 people living in it. It has many historical museums. It is home to the Dixie National Rodeo and Jackson State University. The Hall-of-Fame running back Walter Payton played for Jackson State University.

Biloxi is the second largest city in the state. It is a winter resort city on the **Gulf of Mexico**. It gets many visitors because of its sandy beaches and wonderful resorts. Biloxi is also well known for its wonderful seafood.

Tupelo is a small **manufacturing** city in Mississippi. It is more famous for being the birthplace of the King of Rock-n-Roll, Elvis Presley.

Other splendid cities include Greenville, Hattiesburg, Meridian, Gulfport, Oxford, and Starkville, among others.

Dusk in Jackson, Mississippi. In the foreground is the State Capitol building.

Mississippi's Land

Mississippi has rivers, forests, lakes, hills, farmland, and beaches throughout its land. The state is divided into two very different areas.

The Mississippi Floodplain region is along the western edge of the state alongside the Mississippi River. The land in this region was built up by many floods from both the Mississippi and the Yazoo rivers throughout history.

The Floodplain region between the Mississippi and the Yazoo rivers is known as the Yazoo Basin. The Yazoo Basin is an excellent farming area. In fact, it is one of the most fertile areas in the world.

The other region is the Gulf Coastal Plain. It covers every part of the state except for the far western edge. This region has many different types of land. It has hills, forests, mountains, valleys, prairies, rivers, lakes, and farmland.

This region has sandy beaches at the far bottom of the state and the highest point in Mississippi in the very tip of the northeast corner. Woodall Mountain rises to 806 feet (246 meters) making it the highest point in the state.

Natchez Trace Cypress Swamp near Ross Barnett Reservoir.

Mississippi at Play

Mississippi is a great place to play. There are so many different things to do and see in the state. People are attracted to Mississippi's beautiful land, wonderful sandy beaches, and historic places.

Outdoors, people can go camping, hiking, and sightseeing in the state parks. In the rivers and lakes people enjoy fishing, swimming, and boating. In the southern part of the state are many beaches on the **Gulf of Mexico**. Most people come for the fun in the sun. The warm temperatures are very inviting to people in the north.

People also enjoy museums about the history and art of Mississippi. Some museums are old homes where famous people once lived.

Other popular places that people visit are American **Civil War** battlefield sites. The most famous in the state is Vicksburg National Military Park.

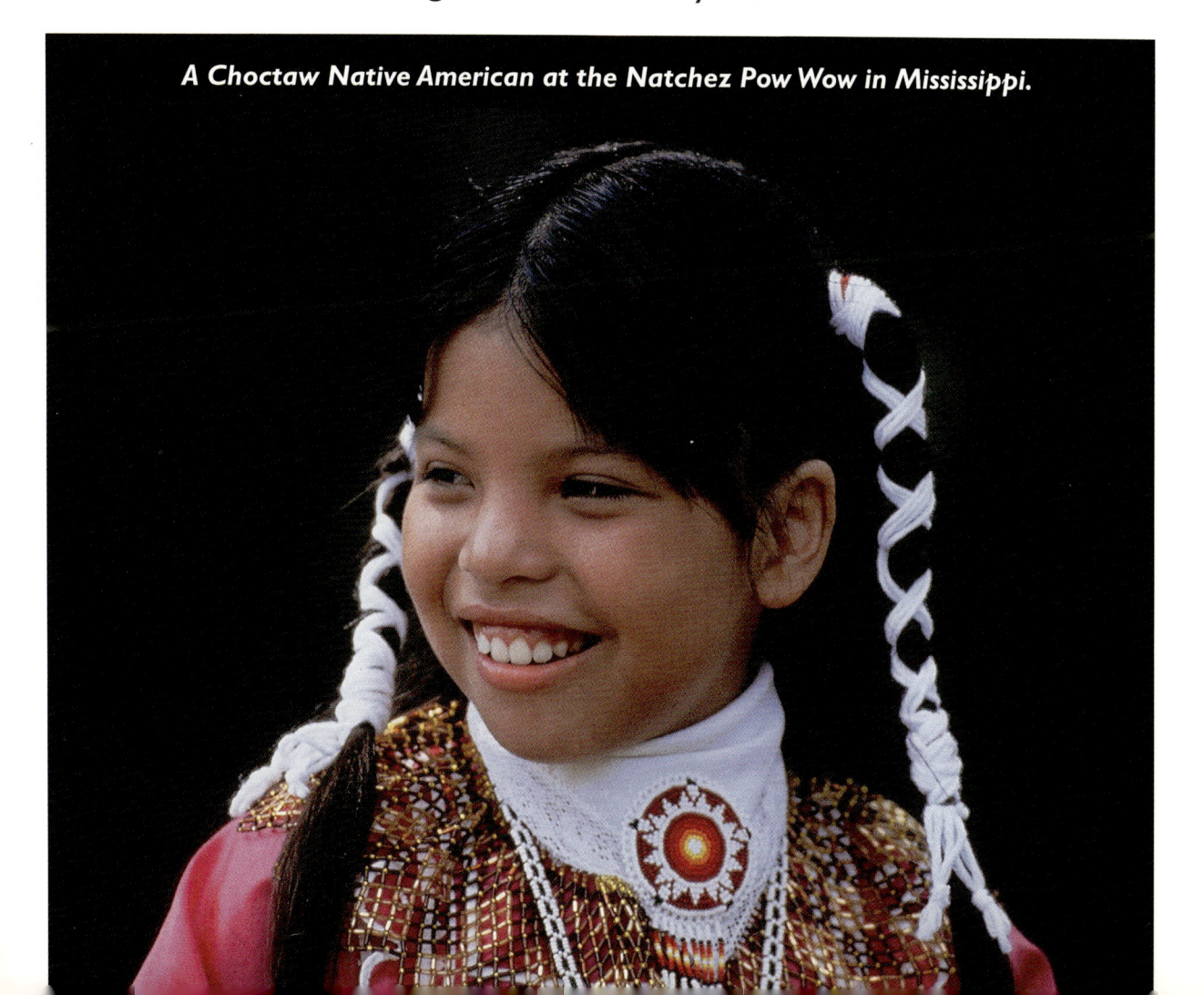

A Choctaw Native American at the Natchez Pow Wow in Mississippi.

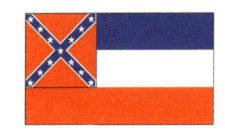

Mississippi at Work

The people of Mississippi must work to make money. There are many different kinds of jobs that people do in the state. Mississippi gets many visitors each year, which makes service jobs very common in the state. Service jobs are working in hotels, resorts, restaurants, and stores.

One out of every four people who work in Mississippi work in some sort of **manufacturing**. At some manufacturing jobs, people make clothes, furniture, wood products, and food products.

Plenty of sunshine and rain have made farming the third biggest **industry** after service and manufacturing. Mississippi has about 38,000 farms. Some of the leading crops grown in the state include hay, corn, oats, cotton, rice, wheat, and soybeans.

Some people in Mississippi are **miners**. **Petroleum** is by far the state's most valuable **mineral**. Other minerals found under the state include **natural gas**, sand, and gravel.

Because of the rivers and the **Gulf of Mexico** many people from Mississippi work in **fisheries**. Of all the catfish caught in the United States, 80 percent comes from Mississippi. Other catches in the state include shrimp, bass, and oysters.

There are many different things to do and see in the great state of Mississippi. Because of its natural beauty, people, land, and warm weather, Mississippi is a great place to visit, live, work, and play.

Fishermen catching catfish in the Mississippi River Delta.

Fun Facts

• The highest point in the state is Woodall Mountain. It is 806 feet (246 meters). The lowest level in the state is sea level.

• The Pascagoula River is a well known place. It is called the Singing River, because it makes mysterious buzzing or singing noises during the night. No one can figure out what makes this sound.

• Mississippi's first road was the historic Natchez Trace. It was developed from a **Native American** trail. The road stretched across the state all the way to Nashville, Tennessee. Today, the 250 mile (402 km) road is one of the most scenic roads in the United States.

• The southern states, including Mississippi, left the United States and started their own country, the Confederate States of America. The first and only president of this country was Jefferson Davis, who was from Mississippi.

The historic Natchez Trace is Mississippi's oldest road.

Glossary

Border: neighboring states, countries, or waters.
Civil Rights Movement: a movement by African Americans to receive equal rights.
Civil War: a war between groups within the same country.
Confederacy: a group that bands together for a common belief. In this case it is the 11 southern states that left the Union between 1860 and 1861.
European: people who originally come from countries in Europe such as England, France, Germany, Italy, etc.
Explorers: people that travel new lands.
Fisheries: the business of catching fish.
Gulf of Mexico: a large bay that borders most of the southern coast of Mississippi.
Industry: big businesses such as factories or manufacturing.
Manufacture: to make things by machine in a factory.
Minerals: things found in the earth, such as rock, diamonds, or coal.
Miners: people who work underground to get minerals.
Native Americans: the first people who were born in and occupied North America.
Natural gas: gas that is found in the earth and is used as fuel.
Petroleum: also known as oil. An oily liquid that is obtained from wells drilled in the ground. It is used to make gasoline, fuel oils, and other products.
Population: the number of people living in a certain place.
Prejudice: an opinion made without taking time and care to judge fairly.
Produce: to make.
Tourism: a business that serves people who are traveling for pleasure, and visiting places of interest.

Internet Sites

Mississippi Online Network
http://msonline.net/main.html
This site has many subjects on Mississippi. Link into books, businesses, clubs, computers, education, games, government, travel, sports, and anything having to do with Mississippi.

Mississippi—The South's Warmest Welcome
http://www.decd.state.ms.us/Tourism.htm
Take a drive through Mississippi and discover one-of-a-kind places that make Mississippi The South's Warmest Welcome.

These sites are subject to change. Go to your favorite search engine and type in Mississippi for more information.

PASS IT ON

Tell Others Something Special About Your State

To educate readers around the country, pass on interesting tips, places to see, history, and little unknown facts about the state you live in. We want to hear from you!
To get posted on ABDO & Daughters website E-mail us at "mystate@abdopub.com"

Index

A
African Americans 11, 18

B
beaches 20, 22, 23, 24
Biloxi 20
British 10

C
cities 20, 21
civil rights 18
Civil War 5, 11, 25
climate 5
college 11
Confederate States 16, 29
cotton state 5
crops 8, 11, 26

D
Davis, Jefferson 16, 29
de Soto, Hernando 10, 12
Dixie National Rodeo 20

E
European 10, 12

F
farming 22, 26
farms 8, 10, 26
fish 9, 24, 27
forests 8, 22, 23
France 10, 12
French explorer 10

G
Gulf of Mexico 4, 6, 8, 9, 20, 22, 24, 27
Gulf States 4

I
industry 5, 11, 26

J
Jackson State University 20

L
La Salle, Robert 10, 12
lakes 22, 23, 24

M
manufacturing 21, 26
minerals 8, 27
Mississippi River 4, 10, 16, 22
Mississippi's land 22
Mississippi's people 18
museums 20, 24

N
NAACP 18
Natchez Trace 28
National Guard 18
Native American 4, 10, 12

P
petroleum 9, 27
population 6, 20, 28

R
railroads 11
rainfall 8
reconstruction 11
rivers 8, 9, 22, 24, 27

S
slavery 5, 11
soil 5, 8
Spanish explorer 10
state capital 6, 20, 29
Supreme Court 16, 18

U
University of Mississippi 14, 18